Living by the Seaside

Richard Spilsbury

www.raintreepublishers.co.uk
Visit our website to find out more information about Raintree books.

To order:
☎ Phone 0845 6044371
🖹 Fax +44 (0) 1865 312263
💻 Email myorders@raintreepublishers.co.uk

Customers from outside the UK please telephone +44 1865 312262

Raintree is an imprint of Capstone Global Library Limited, a company incorporated in England and Wales having its registered office at 7 Pilgrim Street, London, EC4V 6LB - Registered company number: 6695582

Edited by Charlotte Guillain and
  Catherine Veitch
Designed by Joanna Hinton-Malivoire
Original illustrations © Capstone Global Library
Illustrated by Joanna Hinton-Malivoire
Picture research by Elizabeth Alexander and Fiona Orbell
Originated by Dot Gradations Ltd
Printed in China by South China Printing
  Company Ltd

ISBN 978 0 431020 89 1 (hardback)
14 13 12 11 10
10 9 8 7 6 5 4 3 2 1

ISBN 978 0 431020 96 9 (paperback)
15 14 13 12 11 10
10 9 8 7 6 5 4 3 2

British Library Cataloguing in Publication Data
Spilsbury, Richard
Living by the seaside. – (Our local area)
910.9'146-dc22
A full catalogue record for this book is available from the British Library.

Acknowledgements
We would like to thank the following for permission to reproduce photographs: Alamy pp. **8** (© John Boud), **9** (© Chris Rose/BlueSkyStock), **12** (© Justin Kase/zfourz), **13** (© Jack Sullivan), **14** (© Shepic), **15** (© Simon Vine), **17** (© Redsnapper); Collections p. **10** (Michael St. Maur Sheil); Corbis pp. **4** & **5** (© Marc Bedingfield), **6** (© Ric Ergenbright); Getty Images pp. **18** (London Stereoscopic Company), **19** (Mansell/Time & Life Pictures); Photolibrary p. **21** (Erwin Bud Nielsen/Index Stock Imagery); Pictures of Britain pp. **7** (© Deryck Lister Hallam), **11** (© Tony Rostron).

Cover photograph of Ventnor, Isle of Wight, England, UK reproduced with permission of Alamy (© Patrick Eden).

We would like to thank Rachel Bowles for her invaluable help in the preparation of this book.

Every effort has been made to contact copyright holders of material reproduced in this book. Any omissions will be rectified in subsequent printings if notice is given to the publisher.

All the Internet addresses (URLs) given in this book were valid at the time of going to press. However, due to the dynamic nature of the Internet, some addresses may have changed, or sites may have changed or ceased to exist since publication. While the author and publisher regret any inconvenience this may cause readers, no responsibility for any such changes can be accepted by either the author or the publisher.

Contents

Any words appearing in the text in bold, **like this**, are explained in the glossary.

What is the seaside?

The seaside is the land beside the sea. It is sometimes called the **coast**. There are different kinds of seaside. Often at the coast the land stops at **cliffs**. Cliffs are steep slopes of hard and soft rocks that are worn away by the sea waves.

In other places the land meets the sea at beaches. A beach may be covered in mud, sand, rounded pebbles, flat **shingle**, or rocks. Seawater moves up and down a beach every day when the **tide** comes in and goes out again.

Here you can see a sandy beach with rocks at the foot of a steep cliff.

A seaside village

Some people live in villages by the seaside. Some houses in these villages are empty for much of the year. The people who own them live and work somewhere else. They come to the seaside for holidays. Other people live and work in the village all the year round.

Seaside houses are built above the water so they do not get wet.

Where is the harbour entrance?

harbour

lighthouse

seawall

Some seaside villages have a **lighthouse** nearby. This is a tower with lights that warns ships about dangerous rocks. Many seaside villages have a **seawall**, too. This protects the buildings. The seawall also protects any fishing and sailing boats in the **harbour** from the sea when the waves get too rough.

A seaside town

Some people live in seaside towns, and many more people visit these towns to stay for a holiday. Lots of the buildings in a seaside town are for visitors. There are hotels, bed and breakfast places, and caravan sites. But in other ways, seaside towns are just like other towns, with hospitals, libraries, schools, parks, and playing fields.

What different **features** can you see in this seaside town?

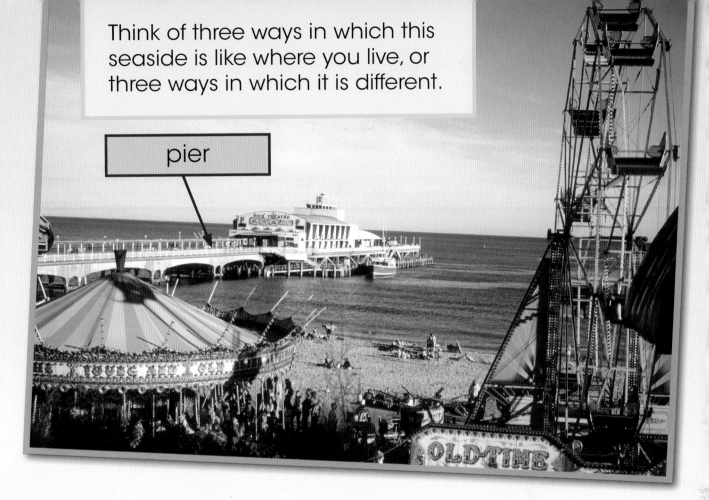

Think of three ways in which this seaside is like where you live, or three ways in which it is different.

pier

Visitors like to walk along the **seafront** on a wide pavement called the **promenade**. In some towns, people can walk out over the sea along the **pier**. They like to visit the **arcades**, cafes, and gift shops along the seafront. They also go to other nearby **attractions**, such as a funfair or gardens.

Seaside jobs

Seaside jobs are often the same as jobs in other local areas. For example, some people are teachers, doctors, or work in small factories. However, some seaside jobs are special. **Lifeguards** keep people safe by the beach and **coastguards** protect people in boats out at sea.

Fishermen catch fish, crabs, and other seafood from boats such as big **trawlers**.

Visitors can buy snacks such as fish and chips at the seaside.

Many people who live by the seaside work in jobs that help visitors. Some people clean and tidy rooms in hotels. Other workers serve food and drinks to people in cafés. Shopkeepers sell gifts and ice creams to visitors. Some people work in theatres and big shops that attract visitors, just like in other towns.

Seaside travel

Visitors travel to the seaside in different ways. Most visitors to small seaside villages go by car because there are no train or bus stations there. People who visit seaside towns may go by bus, coach, ferry boat, or train.

What jobs can you think of that help visitors travel around at the seaside?

At the seaside, people can sometimes travel in unusual ways. Some seaside towns have trams. A tram is a special bus that runs on tracks in the road. Other places have model steam railways. There are also small boats called pedaloes that you move by turning pedals with your feet.

At some beaches you can take donkey rides up and down the sand.

Seaside fun

People have lots of fun at the seaside. In summer, people paddle and swim in the sea. They **surf**, row, and sail boats on the water, too. On the beach, people make sandcastles, eat picnics, and write postcards. Often there are **sand dunes** and hills to climb.

A wetsuit protects this surfer from the Sun and keeps him warm in the cold water.

There is lots of space for exercise on a beach in winter.

In winter, the water is too cold for most people to swim. The waves can be high and rough. People put on scarves and hats to keep warm at the beach. They fly kites, ride horses, walk their dogs, and jog across the sand.

Likes and dislikes

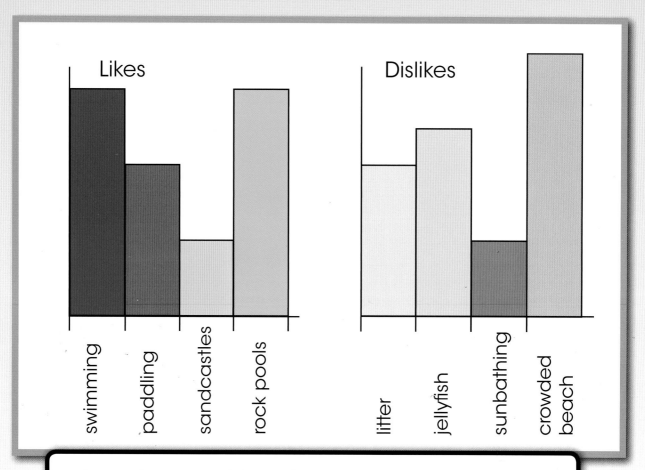

Likes

- swimming
- paddling
- sandcastles
- rock pools

Dislikes

- litter
- jellyfish
- sunbathing
- crowded beach

Jasmine and her friends made a **bar chart**. It shows what the children like and dislike about living by the seaside. What would you like best?

These children are helping to pick up litter that has been brought in by the **tide**.

People do not like litter on beaches because it looks horrible and it can smell. Litter can also harm animals and birds if they eat it or get stuck in it. How could you help to stop people leaving litter?

In the past

The seaside changes in different ways over the years. For example, **piers** get worn away by the sea, and people knock down hotels to build houses on the land. Jobs also change. Long ago, most people in British seaside villages were fishermen. They went out to sea on small wooden fishing boats nearly every day. Today beaches are busy when holidaymakers visit.

This photograph of a beach in Brighton was taken in 1895.

In the past people changed inside bathing carts like these before being wheeled into the sea to swim.

Around 150 years ago, people started to travel to the seaside on steam trains. Later, people came by bus or car. Most people only started to go to the seaside in other countries by aeroplane around 50 years ago. Some old holiday resorts in the United Kingdom (UK) are now much quieter because people take holidays elsewhere.

World coasts

Some countries, such as Austria, have no seaside. They have other countries all around them. Other countries, such as Kenya, have **coast** only on one side. **Islands**, such as the British Isles or Australia, are surrounded by seaside.

Which are the seaside places nearest to your home on this map? Collect together postcards and holiday photos to help you remember which parts of the coast you have visited.

Antarctica South Pole

Many people from the UK visit seasides around the world because the weather and the sea there is warmer than at home. However, some coasts, such as those around Antarctica, are so cold that the top of the sea freezes to ice. People go there to see wildlife such as penguins.

Seaside challenge

This seaside map has squares over it. The squares have letters and numbers that show where things are. For example, the **lighthouse** is in A1. What is in B1 and A4?

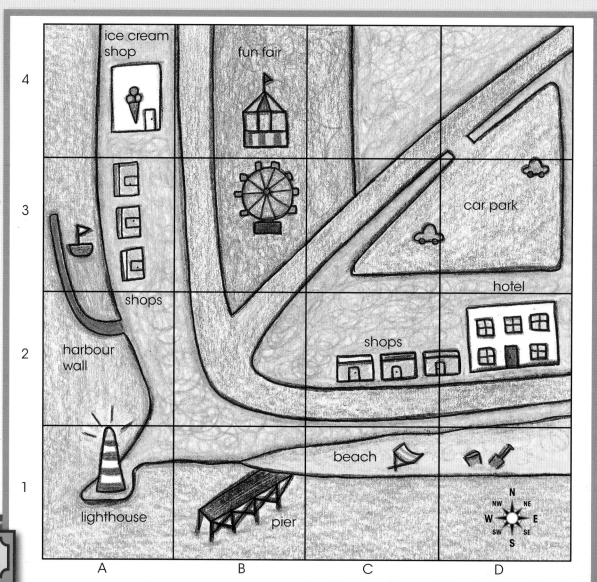

Glossary

arcade tourist attraction with lots of coin-operated machines

attractions things people like to visit, see, or experience such as a zoo

bar chart type of graph where data, such as likes and dislikes, are shown as bars

cliff wide, steep rock face bordering lower land or sea

coast land beside the sea

coastguard person whose job is to keep boats, ships, and people on them safe at sea

features characteristics or appearance of an object or person

harbour place that shelters boats from the sea, or where boats are stored when not in use

island land surrounded by water

lifeguard person whose job is to protect swimmers from accidents

lighthouse tower at the seaside with a powerful light to warn or guide ships at sea

pier raised walkway from land out over water

promenade place where people like to walk, for example by the sea

sand dune hill of sand made by the wind

seafront land running along the sea's edge

seawall wall of stone or concrete built to protect seaside, and buildings there, from powerful waves and flooding

shingle small stones, or gravel, found on a beach

surf to ride the waves on a board

tide regular rise and fall of the height of the sea

trawler large boat that pulls big nets through the sea to catch fish

Index

Find out more

Books to read

Are We There Yet?: My First Holiday, Jen Green and Mike Gordon
(Hodder Children's Books, 2000)

SuperSchemes Unit 01: Around Our School: The Seagulls' Busy Day,
Colin Bridge (Geographical Association, 2005)

Websites

Beside the Seaside
http://home.freeuk.net/elloughton13/seaconte.htm
Visit this site to find out more about UK coastal resorts, such as Blackpool,
the seaside through history, and global seasides. You can even write a
seaside holiday story.